LLŶN – THE PENINSULA'S STORY

The History of North-West Gwynedd

by Michael Senior

ISBN: 0-86381-443-3

First published in 1997 by Gwasg Carreg Gwalch,
12 Iard yr Orsaf, Llanrwst, Wales LL26 0EH
☎ (01492) 642031
Printed and published in Wales.

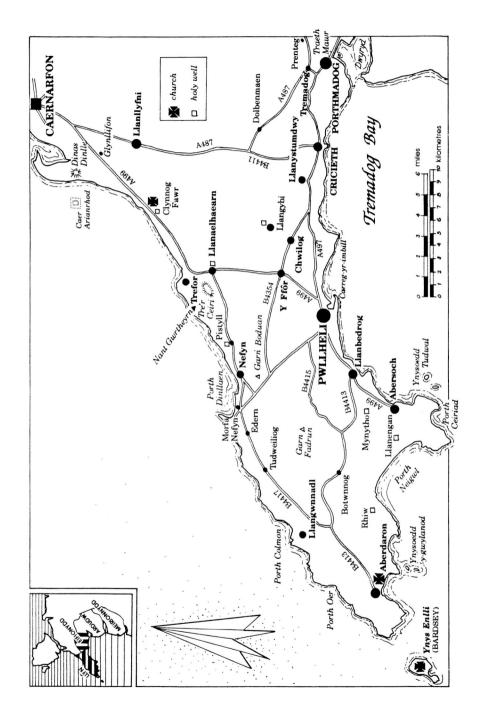

church

holy well

CAERNARFON

Llanllyfni

Glynllifon

Dinas Dinlle

Caer Arianrhod

Clynnog Fawr

A487

Llanaelhaearn

Dolbenmaen

Tremadog

PORTHMADOG

Prenteg

Traeth Mawr

Dwyryd

Llanystumdwy

CRICIETH

Tremadog Bay

Llangybi

Chwilog

A497

A499

B4411

miles

kilometres

Nant Gwrtheyrn

Trefor

Tre'r Ceiri

Pistyll

Nefyn

Garn Boduan

Y Ffôr

Carreg-yr-imbill

PWLLHELI

B4354

Porth Dinllaen

Morfa Nefyn

Edern

Tudweiliog

Garn Fadrun

B4415

B4413

Llanbedrog

Abersoch

Ynysoedd Tudwal

Mynytho

Llanengan

Porth Neigwl

Porth Ceiriad

Porth Colmon

Llangwnnadl

Botwnnog

Rhiw

Aberdaron

Ynysoedd y-gwylland

Porth Oer

Ynys Enlli
(BARDSEY)

LLŶN, GWYNEDD

ARDUDWY

MEIRIONYDD

2

Introduction

The ancient kingdom of Gwynedd has changed its size many times, and recently it has set about changing its status too. At one time it encompassed the start of the Dee valley in the east and approached the English border at Rhuddlan. The Dovey estuary has always formed a natural southern boundary. The more recent county of Gwynedd stopped at the Conwy valley. Now it has shrunk again in size and become one of the new unitary authorities, a sort of large borough incorporating the previous district councils of Arfon, Dwyfor and Meirionnydd. The new county borough of Conwy occupies much of the central area of North Wales, meeting the new Gwynedd on the north coast mid-way between Bangor and Conwy.

A second booklet, companion to this one, 'Meirionnydd's Story', will tell the history of southern Gwynedd. The north coast will fit more easily into the story of the central uplands. Llŷn is a world of its own, and must be treated as such.

Some of the material in this booklet in fact derives from a predecessor which failed to take account of this fact. 'Harlech and Llŷn' really dealt with two separate areas, happening to be at the time the southern part of the administrative area of Gwynedd. The chance is now taken to recognise both their distinctive identities.

Llŷn's individualism is a product, of course, of its geographical isolation, but other factors play a part. Firstly the fact that the Romans do not seem to have depopulated its hillforts indicates that it may have been able to keep a cultural continuity from very ancient times. This has been strengthened by intermarriage, giving rise to a closely linked network of family ties. The feeling of being out on a limb, as is certainly evident from the map, reinforces its population's sense of identity. Their way of life too has only recently begun to change, from the traditional combination of farming and fishing (the sea being all around, and the land intensely rural), to a rather more tourism-geared approach in which they encounter, almost for the first time, people from elsewhere.

There is something much more basic, however, than these historical, economic and social factors. It is the look and feel which the land has. As you reach the soft hills south of Clynnog and approach the Llanaelhaearn valley you get a clear and always recognisable sense of being on Llŷn.

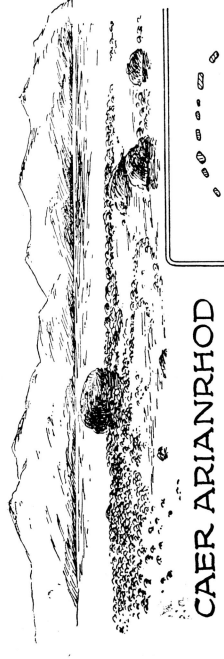

CAER ARIANRHOD

Fig. 45.

Site of Caer Arianrhod, a Roman Fort or Port down to its submergence in the 6th Century. From a photo taken at ebb tide (20ft. 2in.), Aug. 5th, 1909. Crescent of stones (inset) was seen by the writer just below the surface of the water; probably a complete circle. Mountains are Yr Eifl at right and Bwlch Mawr at left hand.

(1) Caer Arianrhod, a sketch and diagram published in 1920

A LAND OF MYTHS

THE evidence available to the archeologist is essentially limited; it consists of things which happen to have been durable enough to have survived. These can provide only a partial picture of the past, and it may help to give this substance if we see it in the context of a record perhaps even more durable and persistent, the remains of the oral tradition.

The stories collected in the book known as 'The Mabinogion' were written down during the Middle Ages, but tell of events of a much earlier period, and may well have been passed down by storytellers from times now effectively lost to us in every other way. They became distorted in the process, of course. But through them we may gain at least an insight into the relative early importance of different areas, and nowhere is this effect more striking than in the area of north-west Gwynedd. This part of the coast of north Wales is exceptionally rich in traditional tales.

Some of these indicate clearly that the coastline has changed. Inundation stories are universal, but the fact that they have a powerful symbolic function does not mean that the inundations to which they have become attached did not occur, and we must at least consider the possibility that not one, but two lost lands lie off this coast.

One of these is said to be in what is now Caernarfon Bay, south-west of the spit, Morfa Dinlle, which forms the mouth of the Menai Strait. A reef of stones known as Caer Arianrhod forms its visible evidence, marked as such on some maps, and located a short distance offshore between Llandwrog and Clynnog (1). It has been recorded and remarked on since the early 17th century, and investigations in the early 20th concluded variously that it was an ancient stone circle, or the ruins of masonry, or (perhaps rather more realistically) a denuded 'drumlin', a lump of land deposited by a glacier from which the encroaching sea has removed the soil, leaving the boulders. At low tide it can be seen from the coast nearby, and stands out as a line of stones of some straightness and evenness, a larger stone in the middle rising above them.

The name means 'Arianrhod's Castle', and it is clearly the place referred to in the story of 'Math, son of Mathonwy', in which the magician Gwydion brought his nephew, Lleu Llaw Gyffes, to confront the latter's malicious mother, Arianrhod. It is interesting to note that 'Caer Arianrhod', as well as being this submerged group of stones, is the Welsh term for the constellation known as the Corona Borealis, and this connection relates Arianrhod directly to the Greek goddess Ariadne, whose silver circlet became that group of stars

(2) *The coastal iron-age fort of Dinas Dinlle has been partly eroded by the sea*

in Greek mythology. We thus perhaps have here an early religious site, the home or 'castle' of the local version of a pan-European goddess.

Right on the border of myth and history lies the story of Macsen, and it lies on the edge of this area of south-west Gwynedd too, being precisely located at the mouth of the river Seiont, the site of the Roman fort of Segontium. It is in itself a delightful tale and of special interest for the way it illustrates how myth distils reality.

The Emperor of Rome took an afternoon sleep on a hot day in the countryside outside the city, where he was hunting. In his sleep he dreamt that he went on a journey; he came to an island, crossed it to its further shore, where he looked onto another island. Below him at the mouth of a river was a castle, and he went down to it. Entering, he was greeted by a beautiful woman, with whom, in his dream, he fell in love. Awaking he found himself absorbed by this love, and likely to pine away. He had messengers sent out in all directions to seek the dreamt-of land.

Eventually they found it. The island was Britain. Crossing it they came to look over Anglesey. There at the mouth of the Seiont was a castle, and going in, sure enough, they found the woman. She declined to go to Rome (not unreasonably sceptical of the story) and suggested that the Emperor come to her. Thus it was that the Romans came to Britain.

The story also features their departure, since the emperor it refers to, by the Welsh name Macsen, was based on Magnus Maximus, a usurper, whose rivalry for the Roman throne eventually led to troops being withdrawn from Britain, and from Segontium outside Caernarfon, in 383 A.D.

In the meantime Segontium had become something of a regional centre, lying as it did right at the western end of the Empire. One significant feature of this is that the Romans appear to have penetrated no further into our area, and this perhaps helps to account for the undeveloped state and independent character of Llŷn. Wherever the Roman roads went and the chain of camps was set up, historically, later progress seeped along the infrastructure. Llŷn remained rural, and self-contained.

The Romans had a camp at Dolbenmaen, in the middle of the base of the peninsula, and a road running from Caernarfon to there, on the route of the present A487; from Dolbenmaen they seem to have got no further, but perhaps curved back to join the main route from Caernarfon to Trawsfynydd and the southward highway in the Ffestiniog valley.

The Llŷn was then, had been for some centuries, a thriving Iron Age community, and because the Romans did not fully colonise it it continued to

(3) An iron-age fort of the promontory type occupies the isthmus behind the bay of Porth Dinllaen

(4) Tre'r Ceiri, 'town of the giants', an iron-age hillfort on the summit of Yr Eifl

8

be so. It is for these reasons that we have there so many fine examples of Iron Age hill forts. Although there are Neolithic cromlechs on the peninsula, such as those at Cefnamwlch and the long chambered cairn in the area of Rhiw, they are more frequent further south in Gwynedd; and (to generalise) it seems that the Harlech hinterland, the land known historically as Ardudwy, was a centre of activities in the Neolithic and Bronze Ages, and the Llŷn more important in the Iron Age. Just as six neolithic tombs stand within a few miles of each other in Ardudwy, so Llŷn boasts a surprising cluster of prime examples of Iron Age forts. From Dinas Dinlle in the north, on the coast near Llandwrog, via Tre'r Ceiri, Porth Dinllaen and Garn Boduan to Garn Fadrun, is altogether seventeen miles, and these were the equivalent in their time of major towns. South of Garn Fadrun yet another fort occurs at Pen y Gaer, west of Abersoch.

Due to the constant conflict of the sea with the land, only half of the ring fort of Dinas Dinlle (2) is left. The rest has fallen into the sea. Standing on top of it you can see on the beach below the rounded, even stones which once composed it. It is a remarkably large and steep mound in this generally flat, low-lying area, and must always have been a prominent landmark.

Legend, and its name, connect the fort with Lleu Llaw Gyffes, whom we met in connection with his mother's seat, Caer Arianrhod, which lies not far offshore from here. Gwydion and Lleu are described as walking on the seashore near Aber Menai, and the fort is specifically named as the place where Lleu grew up. Many other place-names in the area reflect the connection of this part of Gwynedd with these characters.

Dates for such structures are vague, and to say that it belongs to the Iron Age places its occupation from perhaps the early years B.C. up to the period of the Roman invasion. Finds of Roman coins indicate that it was still in use in the 2nd and 3rd centuries A.D.

These ringed forts are normally on hilltops, and Dinlle is unusual in having been built on what was probably a glacial deposit overlooking a convenient landing place. Its neighbour at Dinllaen, we shall see, is in a similar position, and both perhaps remind us more of the promontory forts of Ireland than of North Wales' more common hillfort version.

The fact that Dinlle (like several other forts) has a double rampart – an outer wall halfway up its slope, an inner one surrounding its broad top – is seen by some as evidence of two periods of use, a rebuilding or improvement being carried out after the fort had been taken, or occupied after being abandoned, by an invading force.

(4) Section of the wall-walk at Tre'r Ceiri

(4) Hut inside the enclosed area

No legendary traditions attach to the similar fort at Dinllaen (3), but its position and style make it seem likely to have been the work of the same people. It too overlooks a convenient landing place. In this case full use is made of the isthmus site, since the fort occupies the narrow neck of the peninsula. It has been partly damaged by the construction of the golf course and by the cutting of a road down to the buildings on the shore. Due to the occupation of the whole headland by the golf club, Porth Dinllaen as a whole is not accessible to the public by car, but when the tide is out there is a pleasant walk along the beach.

These remains, and indeed almost everything of the period which one finds in North Wales, seem sparse and modest when one comes to Tre'r Ceiri, the 'town of the giants' (4). It stands on the easternmost of the three peaks known as the Rivals, a corruption of the Welsh name, Yr Eifl *(two forks)*. Finds here have indicated a period of use at least up to the end of the 4th century A.D., starting from sometime in the mid-second. These are all we have evidence for, but the presence of an apparently bronze-age cairn at the summit of the hill which the ramparts enclose indicates earlier uses of the site. The point which is of interest is that the occupation of all these forts overlapped, and whether they were inhabited by the same group of people or by groups of different origins there remains a compelling conclusion from their size and their proximity: in and around the 3rd century A.D. Llŷn was remarkably densely populated.

Tre'r Ceiri is huge. The buildings themselves are not giant-like, nor even particularly large for their period, but the extent of the site is certainly impressive. Within its 950-feet by 340-feet enclosure there are the remains of some 150 huts. The features that make Tre'r Ceiri unusual are this extensiveness and the state of preservation of its structures. It looks in fact quite recently built, perhaps temporarily vacated. Whether this is because of a higher quality of construction than usual, or because the remoteness of its position has made it less vulnerable to interference it is hard to say. Certainly many lower forts have suffered from the effects of later works and of farming. On the other hand Tre'r Ceiri does give the impression of being somehow better built: the faced walls of the huts, the battlements with, on the seaward side, their wall-walk still in place, they all display a confidence on the part of their makers in the perfection of their skills.

Its state of preservation also makes it particularly valuable as an illustration of how such Iron Age structures would have looked when they were new: the wall-walks and the incurving walls of the huts are features to

(5) Nant Gwrtheyrn, now a Welsh-learners' centre

(6) Garn Boduan

bear in mind when visiting more ruined forts.

The fact that Tre'r Ceiri stands around the summit of a steeply-sided mountain of 1,500 feet is sufficient to ration the number of people who see it. It is, in fact, well worth the effort. Not only is there the experience of stepping into the world of a millennium and a half ago, but there is also a view of a great deal of North Wales.

One of the most remarkable things in this area crowded with impressive artefacts is a natural feature. Nant Gwrtheyrn, however, has a tenuous but appealing link with history (5). Its name connects it with the high-king of the Britons, Vortigern, who is blamed by early historians for facilitating the Saxon invasion. It is a well-established tradition that when the situation deteriorated the high-king fled to North Wales. At Dinas Emrys, above Beddgelert, he is said to have tried to build a castle. This startlingly steep and isolated ravine, 'Vortigern's valley', was his second and last place of refuge.

There is some indication in the lore that after his failure, and in effect capitulation, arising as they did out of error or folly, Vortigern was in need of protection against his own people as well as the invaders. He could not have picked a better spot to ensure isolation from the whole world than Nant Gwrtheyrn. Hanging valleys on enclosing cliffs rear vertiginously over a plainly exclusive zone. You look down into it, but the height and the steepness discourage entry.

There are as it happens many signs of ancient habitation in the valley and around it, although the mound called Castell Gwrtheyrn is probably natural. Until about 1700 there apparently stood on this outcrop a stone burial chamber complete with its covering mound, known as Bedd Gwrtheyrn, 'Vortigern's grave'. According to Pennant, writing in the 1770's, the locals excavated it themselves and discovered the bones of a tall man in a stone coffin. "This gives a degree of credibility to the tradition," he said, "especially as no other bodies were found near the cairn . . . which affords a proof at least of respect to the rank of the person . . . "

There are early hut circles and long huts in and around the valley, and when Pennant visited it it was farmed by three families, so that in spite of its obvious inhospitableness it seems to have been inhabited continuously from prehistory. During the last century it became a quarrying village, and as the quarry industry declined its isolation led to gradual depopulation until its few houses stood empty. In more recent times this rather unreal place has been acquired by a trust to form the National Language School, providing a successful centre for the teaching of Welsh – an appropriate recompense,

(6) Hut circles in Garn Boduan hill-fort

(7) Garn Fadrun, site of another iron-age hillfort

perhaps, for Vortigern's ancient mistake.

Five miles from Tre'r Ceiri is a fort of a similar size, Garn Boduan, also on a steep high hill (6). Most visible of the remains here is the small citadel-like fort on the summit, of Roman or sub-Roman date and apparently an addition to the main compound, which itself falls into two periods represented by its two distinct ramparts. These apparently enclose the remains of 170 huts, clusters of which are easy to see on the southern edge of the plateau. The fort is undoubtedly large and has an extensive view over the coastal plain, a breathtaking spread of field patterns and lanes, with the headlands of Penrhyn Nefyn and Porth Dinllaen on one side and the hills of the peninsula stretching away on another. Although some of the huts are unusually large, they are not as impressive or prominent as those of Tre'r Ceiri.

Less than four miles separates Garn Boduan from Llŷn's other notable hillfort. Right down the end of the peninsula, Garn Fadrun is impressive for itself, its situation and eminence, rather than for its structures (7). the enclosed area of the round mountain's flat summit is in all about 26 acres, and if anything feels larger. There are signs of the remains of a bronze-age cairn, as at Tre'r Ceiri, indicating perhaps that almost every summit had a burial of that time; the south-western area particularly is thick with the stones of huts and structures, but none well-preserved; an inner, and apparently older wall again indicates two different periods of occupation; on the summit (as at Garn Boduan) are the walls of a later structure, in this case probably medieval. It might not have been worth the trip for the experience of these things, but in one respect Garn Fadrun is pre-eminent. It would be worth a much harder climb to gain the benefit of such a view.

Struck out at the end of Wales yet surrounded by its branching coastline, Garn Fadrun provides a kind of summary of all that is most remarkable about this extraordinary landscape. The heaped mountains of Snowdonia roll on one side into their banks of cloud. The estuaries and their surrounding foothills step southwards on another. Far across the bay we look to South Wales, where the Pembrokeshire coast juts expansively into the Irish Sea. The coast of Anglesey and Holy Island and sometimes, beside and beyond them, the Irish hills, enclose the remaining horizon. Such a spread and such variety of view can surely be found in few other places.

EARLY CHRISTIANS

WWHEN the Romans left a long period of unsettled conditions resulted for which records are sparse. Though we know of this as the 'Dark Ages' it must not be assumed to be by any means empty of events. In this part of North Wales raids from across the Irish Sea were the initial problem, and we may guess that in places the ineffectiveness of resistance to these led to colonisation. There may indeed have been an element of earlier affinity. Ireland and the Llŷn are after all within sight of one another. Indeed the very name, until recently spelt 'Lleyn', (now adapted to conform to the way it has come to be pronounced), confirms a close Irish connection, since it comes from the same root as Leinster.

Elsewhere in Britain the trouble came not from the west but from the continent of Europe. Although it took some time to penetrate into this fastness, its effects came ahead of it.

One major change which had come about during the sub-Roman period was the spread of Christianity. In its early western form this took a monastic nature, small communities of religious people being based on a sacred settlement under the auspices of a missionary leader, whose name often survives in church dedications as an area's local saint.

Such communities favoured remoteness, and that factor became more important as Saxon raids on Christian sites in the border country and mid-Wales uprooted and intimidated the monks who had previously flourished there. Remoteness is one quality the Llŷn peninsula had to offer, once the focus of danger had shifted eastwards, and nowhere is it better exemplified than on the island of Bardsey (8).

As early as the beginning of the 6th century St Cadfan, ousted from Brittany, had founded a monastery there. As troubles elsewhere increased it became the refuge of other holy men, and dispossessed communities of monks flocked there during the 7th century. Thus it was that it came to be regarded as an especially sacred place.

Giraldus Cambrensis (who toured North Wales with Archbishop Baldwin in 1188) records that the island was remarkably free from disease, and says that "very many bodies of saints are said to be buried there". It was evidently after his time that the legend grew that the number of these was 20,000. To be the burial place of a single saint gave a religious spot much prestige, and qualified it as the destination of pilgrimage. To be the reputed burial-place of 20,000 raised this island to a unique position, and in terms of

(8) Bardsey island   17

(8) Bardsey island from Mynydd Mawr

(9) Clynnog Fawr, main church on the pilgrim route

medieval merit three pilgrimages to Bardsey were the equivalent of one to Rome.

Hence it ws that a pilgrim route grew up, as influential on the area then as a tourist itinerary is today. A number of substantial churches grew along the route, where pilgrims might pause for both devotion and sustenance. Starting with Clynnog Fawr (9), the largest and greatest of these, we have a chain stretching in easy stages: Llanaelhaearn, Pistyll, Nefyn, Edern, Tudweiliog, Penllech, Llangwnnadl, Aberdaron. Some of these are truly notable.

Clynnog itself is famous for its magnificence, a late-15th century building largely extended in the early 16th. It is said to have been founded by St Beuno, patron of many North Wales churches, in the 7th century, and a 16th-century chapel linked to the main church by a passage encloses the supposed spot of the original foundation. Beuno himself was said to have been buried there in the late 7th century. The monastery which he founded served the pilgrim travellers through the Middle Ages, and remained as a religious community even after the Dissolution of the Monasteries.

Beuno was a saint associated with healing, and a story connecting him with St Winifred's Well at Holywell shows him as being able to cure even decapitation. Winifred had her head cut off by the local king, and Beuno successfully stuck it back on. St Winifred (as she then became) went on to live another 15 years. Pennant records that on his visit to Clynnog in the 1770's Beuno's tomb (now no longer apparent) was a resort of the sick:

> In the midst is the tomb of the saint, plain, and altar-shaped. Votaries were wont to have great faith in him, and did not doubt but that by means of a night's lodging on his tomb, a cure would be found for all diseases. It was customary to cover it with rushes, and leave on it till morning sick children, after making them first undergo ablution in the neighbouring holy well; and I myself once saw on it a feather bed, on which a poor paralytic from Meirioneddshire had lain the whole night, after undergoing the same ceremony.

The church, says Pennant, "is the most magnificent structure of its kind in North Wales", and it would be hard to disagree. He tells us also of the legend that all calves and lambs born with 'Beuno's mark', "a certain natural mark in the ear", were delivered as offerings to the church, being sold by the churchwardens to effect repairs. The custom apparently continued in his day. The medieval chest in which they kept the funds in the meantime, 'Beuno's

(10) St Beuno's church at Pistyll

(10) 12th century font with ancient Celtic pattern

chest', may still be seen in the church.

Another Beuno church, but very different in style, is that at Pistyll (10). The area of the farm by the church was a hospice for pilgrims, and the monks grew hops and fruit in the surrounding area and, in the healing tradition inherited from Beuno, medicinal herbs, some of which still survive in the churchyard.

St Beuno's church at Pistyll is evidence of the power of simplicity, its old stonework and plain rectangular plan creating an atmosphere of peace and harmony as effectively as might any louder statement. Its present structure is largely original, probably dating from the 12th century with a slight eastern extension in the 15th. A fine font of 12th-century date bears a Celtic image of endlessness, intertwined strands similar to those of the 'endless knot'. Until it was slated in the last century the church was thatched, and the rope-holes by which the thatched roof was secured can be seen in its timbers. The entrance to an earlier form of the building – perhaps even that founded in the 7th century by Beuno – may be seen in the form of steps jutting from the base of the south wall. A corner-stone of this older building is also visible in the eastern part of the north wall, and another early feature is the lepers' window, by which lepers outside the church might see the altar and the elevation of the host.

A contrast to Pistyll again is the striking perpendicular-style church of Llangwnnadl (11). One does not expect this elevated style in something so small, associating it rather with grander structures. Here it is most effective, and gives to Llangwnnadl (a name contracted from its dedication to St Gwynhoedl) a very pleasant lightness and air of uplift. The fact that the church dates mainly from the 1520's and '30's (although its original foundation, like that of all the others in this area, is of the dark-age period) is evidence of the success and longevity of use of the pilgrim route. The two extra aisles were added to an old rectangular structure, now the central aisle, at this period, the north aisle first and the south some ten years later. These effects of the great popularity of this resting place on the journey give to the church now its most unusual shape and spaciousness.

The culmination of the journey must have been the arrival at Aberdaron, where the church of St Hywyn stands at the very edge of the shore, its graveyard protected from an aggressive sea by a strong defensive wall (12).

Aberdaron church is mainly of the early 16th century, though the Norman doorway is original and that part of the west wall surrounding it and the north wall adjoining are of the 12th century. The earlier pilgrims'

(11) The church of St Gwynhoedl at Llangwnnadl

(12) Aberdaron church

oratory, dating back to the 6th century, the time when Cadfan (to whom St Hywyn, Aberdaron's patron, was confessor) founded the original settlement on Bardsey, would have been made of wood, and this structure, like so many others, represents part of the great programme of church-building in stone which took place in a Norman style in the settled and relatively prosperous period of the first half of the 12th century. A curious feature of St Hywyn's today is that the build-up of sand has raised the level of the surrounding churchyard so that the interior of the church seems to be below ground.

There is very little to see now on Bardsey Island (in Welsh, Ynys Enlli) itself of the great medieval monastery which must have stood there. Pennant describes an oratory and the Abbot's house, although, by then even, the religious community was a part of a distant past, Bardsey's spiritual life being "under the care of a single rustic," a place which "once afforded, during life, an asylum to 20,000 saints; and after death, graves to as many of their bodies."

The pilgrims left from a cove a little south of Aberdaron, called Porth Meudwy (13), but now the official route is from Pwllheli, from where there are organised trips during the summer in suitable weather. The island became almost depopulated, but is now returning to life as a nature reserve. The buildings there today are farms built in the 19th century; the crumbling remains of the tower of the abbey church is all that is left of the monastery (14). The early Celtic foundation had become Augustinian in the 13th century, suffered Dissolution in the 16th, and its buildings fell to ruins in the 19th century.

A lighthouse kept the island inhabited from 1821, and in the 1970's a new farming community was established by Lord Newborough, whose family owned the island for generations. The Newboroughs, descended from the Glyns, or Glynnes, of Glynllifon (15), near Llandwrog, had married into the Wynn family in about 1700, and came to be owners of a considerable spread of property. Indeed their Glynllifon estate extends over this end of the peninsula. The present house of Glynllifon (now an agricultural college) was built between 1836 and 1848 on the site of an 18th century house which had burnt down, the Newborough title, an Irish peerage, having been created in 1776.

(13) Porth Meudwy, sailing place of the pilgrims

(14) Bardsey: remains of the abbey and the farm buildings

24

(15) Glynllifon, seat of the Newborough family

CRICIETH

URING the whole of this period, from the departure of the Romans through the early Middle Ages, North Wales had been ruled by independent princes. The castle at Cricieth, for instance, was not among those originally built by Edward I, although he strengthened it and used it. (16) It was one of the seats of the princes of Gwynedd, becoming the administrative centre of the commote of Eifionydd in the reign of Llywelyn the Great. Before that Eifionydd had been ruled from the old Roman centre of Dolbenmaen, connected as that was to the greater world by the Roman road to Caernarfon. There was a small medieval motte-and-bailey castle there. It was Llywelyn who moved this centre southwards down the river Dwyfor to Cricieth. That was in the 1230's.

Llywelyn's castle forms the inner ward of the complex which we see today, a striking innovation of it being the D-shaped towers. These follow the new fashion in castle-building of the time, and may have been influenced by the castle built at Montgomery by the Norman baron Hubert de Burgh, which Llywelyn would undoubtedly have known. The D-shaped towers flank a heavily protected gatehouse. The solid structure on its conspicuous eminence proclaims, from the start, Llywelyn's determination to maintain a strong grip on Eifionydd, and in due course on North Wales.

Once built, Cricieth, like all castles, attracted the more colourful elements of history. The background to the situation at the close of Wales's period of independence is complicated by a rivalry within the ruling family. Llywelyn the Great had ruled for more than twenty years and achieved a considerable degree of unity. When he died, in 1240, there was dispute over the succession. His elder son Gruffudd was illegitimate, though possibly favoured by the people since his legitimate son Dafydd, whom he himself wished to be heir, was half English, being the son of the Princess Joan, daughter of King John. Anticipating danger, Dafydd had Gruffudd and his son Owain imprisoned in Cricieth castle.

That was in 1239. Gruffudd spent two more years in Cricieth, until in 1241 Dafydd was beaten in battle by Henry III, who took the hapless Gruffudd to London with him on the basis of supporting his claim to territory in North Wales. In fact Gruffudd remained a prisoner, and he died in the process of trying to escape from the Tower of London.

It was not the last time this secure little fortress has been put to such a use. Dafydd did not rule Wales for long, and the succession reverted to the alternative line. The next, and last, of the independent princes was Llywelyn

(16) Cricieth castle   27

(16) Cricieth castle on its headland

ap Gruffudd. He similarly found it necessary to imprison a threatening rival, Maredudd, the heir of the South Wales dynasty, and he too used Cricieth castle for this purpose, in 1259. Indeed he seems to have made it his headquarters, since he wrote to Edward I from there in the 1270's. The latter came to Cricieth during his invasion in the 1280's, but decided against making it one of his major castles. He founded a borough around it, which was to a large extent to determine the form of its future importance. Edward also improved the inner gatehouse by rebuilding the battlements, which were raised again later by his son. On the whole, however, what we have rearing above us now is mainly the work of the two Llywelyns.

Llywelyn ap Gruffudd enlarged his grandfather's basic keep by adding to it an outer ward. He also threw round the whole an outer curtain wall, at two of the extremities of which he placed large square towers. In this finished form Cricieth castle was fit to continue its role in history.

This for a time promised to be greater than the eventual reality. Edward I had originally intended the formation of two shires, in place of what became, in the final version of the Statute of Rhuddlan, Caernarfonshire: one based at Conwy, the other at Cricieth. If Criciethshire had ever come into existence the fate of this essentially modest place would have been different, and the area it covered (the Llŷn and the southern part of Gwynedd as far as Llanbedr) might have played a greater part in North Wales's later history. Instead Edward finally only founded a borough, with, as elsewhere, the constable of the castle as mayor. Unusually Cricieth remained unwalled, though the castle remained for a time defensible. It was besieged by Welsh rebels in the 1290's during the revolt of Madog ap Llywelyn, and relieved by Edward I himself. He had, on adopting it as a royal castle, carried out extensive rebuilding, changing the form of the towers at the south-west and south-east sides of the complex, and extended the outer gatehouse. He rebuilt and raised the battlements of the inner gatehouse, and, it seems likely, added a further floor to the towers he repaired. The work was largely due to the damage he himself had inflicted on the castle in taking it in the first place, and later work may have succeeded Madog's siege. Cricieth castle owes its later state of ruin to the systematic destruction carried out by Owain Glyndŵr, when, having captured it, he set it on fire.

It is to the period of Edward's borough that Cricieth's oldest building after the castle, the Parish Church, belongs. (17) The southern aisle of St Catherine's is the older, the equal-sized northern part being added during early Tudor times. There is no evidence, but the conclusion that the site

(17) Cricieth church

(18) The old borough below the castle

predates Edward's arrival seems inevitable. It is too far away from the castle to have been in the small clustered borough which Edward founded, which huddled at the castle's feet. The whole church was much restored in 1872.

The borough Edward founded consisted of the streets near to the castle, and for centuries Cricieth remained no more than this. (18) Noted for its herring fishery, it remained comparatively isolated in the scheme of North Wales communications until the reclamation of Traeth Mawr and the consequent causeway linked it to the south, in the second decade of the last century. In 1537 Leland had described it as "decayed", and even at the beginning of the last century its population remained as low as four hundred people. By the middle of that century things were looking up slightly, and the population reached eight hundred. Black's 'Picturesque Guide' was still describing it in 1866 as a "small insignificant place". It was the coming of the railway shortly after that which turned it into a resort. The 'Thorough Guide' for 1895 describes it as "a pleasant little spot" which is "growing in favour", and by 1909 it is "now deservedly enjoying a rapidly-growing reputation". The population then was 1,405, not far short of its current level.

As an old borough Cricieth had in the meantime played its part politically as an important element of 'Caernarfon Boroughs', the parliamentary seat to which a young Cricieth solicitor, David Lloyd George, was elected in 1890 by a mere eighteen votes.

QUARRIES AND SCHOONERS

WHEN Thomas Pennant made his journey through North Wales in the 1770's he recorded that the rural part of Llŷn was at that time something of a backwater. "The houses of the common people are very mean; made with clay, thatched, and destitute of chimnies." The land was largely undeveloped, grazing ground for its main agricultural product, Welsh Black cattle. It was, Pennant records, "neglected for the sake of the herring-fishery."

Pennant's implication of a conflict between the two industries, fishing and farming, it however probably an exaggeration. They have always been complementary in the Llŷn, and indeed remain so to this day. In fact the two industries in combination provided a sustantial source of income during the 18th century, although it must have been unevenly distributed if it left 'the common people' in the plight in which Pennant found them. By the end of the century Llŷn was exporting cattle to the number of about 6,000 head a year, and in the year 1747 some 5,000 barrels of herring were exported from the port of Nefyn alone. It is perhaps the ability of the region to survive by these means at a time when other areas were developing trade and industry that has kept Llŷn as rural and unaltered as it is today.

At the same time it is clear that Llŷn as a whole had deteriorated economically by the 18th century, from a relatively greater prosperity in medieval and Tudor times, probably largely because of the long neglect of its roads and the consequent barrier to communications formed by its distinctly rugged terrain.

Pwllheli and Nefyn, the two main towns and ports of the peninsula, are by no means without history. They had both been given their charters by the Black Prince, acting as Prince of Wales, in 1355, in recognition of their (then) trading importance; and the latter was the site chosen by Edward I for the tournament with which he celebrated his conquest of Gwynedd in 1284. This seems a strange choice, and one must suppose that Edward wished to stage the event as deep as possible within the western heartland of Gwynedd. Nefyn, however, was a centre of local administration, the 'maerdre' of its commote, and one of the seats of Welsh princes. A Norman motte on the north-west side of the town reminds us that it then became an anglicized borough, and as such it was in due course destroyed by Owain Glyndŵr, a fate from which it has never really recovered. The motte is

(19) The natural harbour of Porth Dinllaen nearly became the main port for Ireland

(20) Trefor quarry

(20) The quarry-men's cottages at Trefor village

crowned by a probably 19th century watchtower, thought to be connected to the one-time flourishing herring fishery.

Pwllheli was a fishing port of some importance by the 16th century, and is mentioned by Pennant as "the best town in this country". It had become a ship-building centre during the 18th century, and continued in this industry into the 19th until it was outstripped and in the end eclipsed by the new town of Port Madoc, by 1880. In the meantime a harbour had been constructed in the early 19th century which gave rise to reclaimed land in the area where the road to Llanbedrog then ran.

By then several events which radically altered the balance of the area had taken place. During the first half of the 19th century the issue of the official port for Ireland was still undecided, and although investment in the harbour of Holyhead would seem to have prejudiced the decision, the problem of constructing a crossing of the Straits for a time diverted interest to the natural harbour of Porth Dinllaen (19). The route through Montgomeryshire to the Llŷn would probably have been more direct than that eventually chosen, and would have avoided the obstacle of the mountains. Even when in the 1820's the Menai Strait was successfully crossed by Telford's bridge, the matter was not finally settled, and optimistic would-be entrepreneurs continued to build suitable inns along the route, through Tremadoc and Chwilog, which they imagined the new road would take.

If all this seems surprising to us now, we must remember that Porth Dinllaen in fact had a long history already as a port for Ireland. Its rivalry with Holyhead can be traced back to the 17th century. Eventually the matter was decided officially as late as 1839, and even then the decision depended on a casting vote. Looking at it now, a tiny hamlet isolated on its headland, one's imagination is stretched by the thought of how different the scene would be, and the whole layout of North Wales' communications and settlements, if the decision had gone the other way.

In the meantime the possibility had affected other issues. Samuel Holland, whose family were to rise to prominence as developers of the Ffestiniog quarries, started quarrying stone on Yr Eifl with a view to supplying the construction of the proposed new harbour. In spite of the failure of its purpose, the quarry thrived, and a flourishing industry had developed in that area by 1850. The purpose-built village of Trefor (20), named after Holland's foreman, Trevor Jones, is the surviving evidence of this, although the quarry works themselves are now abandoned. Further

(21) Slate quay on the river Dwyryd

(22) Traeth Mawr, the land reclaimed by Madocks

quarrying outlets, each with its own pier, emerged down the inaccessible coast nearby, on the shores of the roadless hills between Trefor and Pistyll. The stone (an amalgam of quartz and porphyrite, not strictly granite) had more limited use than that of the rival works at Penmaenmawr, being sought-after for a time for monumental purposes and for making curling stones, its range of colours making it decorative as well as functional.

Although stone has been a major export along this coast at certain times, it cannot rank in importance in the area's economy in the same league as slate. The Llŷn peninsula possesses no great slate quarries itself, but has inevitably been much affected historically by the vast and abundant works at Ffestiniog.

The urbanisation taking place around Britain and the newly industrial countries of Europe at the end of the 18th century led to a surge in the demand for roofing slates, for which North Wales happened to possess the ideal raw material. The price of slates doubled between the years 1798 and 1825. There had been a trade in roofing slates in North Wales since the 16th century, and the Ffestiniog quarries themselves were in operation by the end of the 18th. It was largely the arrival of the young Samuel Holland to take over the management of his father's disordered business, in 1821, that stimulated Ffestiniog's rise to prominence. By 1825 its output had increased to about 10,000 tons.

At that time the slates were brought down a rough track on pack animals, transferred in the Vale of Ffestiniog into carts, and shipped into small boats on the river Dwyryd at a point where it is tidal, by which means they sailed down the river until it met the Glaslyn, and loaded their cargoes onto larger ships at mooring alongside the sand-dunes which form the coast between Borth-y-Gest and Morfa Bychan. The quays either side of the Dwyryd where the slates were first shipped – substantial stone structures of alternating platforms and steps – can still be seen, in many places still in excellent condition (21).

In the 1820's, however, these activities, and the area as a whole, were in the process of undergoing radical change, largely as a result of the will and determination of one man. William Alexander Madocks came from a family which owned property near Wrexham, where they were old-established landowners. His father was a successful barrister, however, and he himself was born in London, in 1773. In due course he inherited some of the Denbighshire estates and enough capital to build himself a house near Dolgellau, where he combined a vigorous social life with his legal practice in London.

(23) Madock's first embankment, near Tremadog

(24) Tremadog town square

QUARRIES AND SCHOONERS

Landscape improvement was a fashion of the time, and Madocks was by nature a creator, more suited to being a landscape architect and designer than a lawyer. When he started buying small farms in the neighbourhood of Penmorfa, in the 1790's, it was probably with an interest in the landscape rather than agriculture. Reclamation of the shores of the estuary had already started, as part of the widespread enclosure movement, itself caused by the agricultural revolution and consequent rise in land values. Madocks' schemes developed gradually from this, but were probably ambitious from the start.

The reclamation of Traeth Mawr (22) was not a new idea, as no doubt he knew. A scheme for reclaiming much of the estuary had been devised by Sir John Wynn (whose family originated from these parts) in 1625. Sir John was advised against it, and the project never started. Madocks however was not so easily daunted.

Part of the point of reclaiming Traeth Mawr was to do with communications, and in this the question of the port for Ireland again affected the course of events. From the days recounted by the Mabinogion onwards there had been a low-tide crossing over the sands, saving a long journey round the big inlet. A route to Porth Dinllaen from mid-Wales would avoid the problems of ferries at both Conwy and the Menai Strait, but it would come up against the equally severe difficulty of the crossing of Traeth Mawr. It was, says Pennant, "of most dangerous passage to strangers, by reason of the tides which flow here with great rapidity". The Act of Union with Ireland (effective from January 1801), which involved Irish M.P.'s travelling regularly to Westminster, made the issue of national importance; and Madocks himself, who was Member of Parliament for Boston in Lincolnshire from 1802, helped to steer a bill through Parliament to provide the Porth Dinllaen Harbour Company, formed in 1806, with funds to build a harbour.

In the meantime his reclamation schemes were already under way. Over the course of five years he had constructed an embankment stretching from where Porthmadog now is to a point on the Beddgelert road near the hamlet of Prenteg (which may still be seen running over the fields) (23), and by 1800 he had succeeded in extending his property by this means by some 2,000 acres.

On this first area of reclamation he then built a fine small town, in an 18th century style, which he called Tremadoc (24). Although the name is undoubtedly intended to recall his own, it had the historical justification that it was traditionally the starting point of the voyage of Prince Madoc (or

(25) Porthmadog harbour now

(26) The Porthmadog Brigantine, Edward Windus,
at Hamburg about 1900

Madog, in its more correct form), the 12th-century Welsh explorer who was said to have been one of the first to reach America. The island from which he is reputed to have set sail is now a rocky wooded outcrop, still called after him Ynys Fadog, to the left of the road which leaves Tremadog for Porthmadog (as the names are now spelt).

Madocks improved the house above this area, Tan-yr-Allt, which he made his home. He designed both this and much of Tremadog himself, sending detailed instructions and sketches from London when he was kept there on Parliamentary business. The town hall, which housed a theatre, is much studied for its style, and the Gothic church and impressive Peniel chapel are also interesting specimens. The new town was incidentally destined to an unforeseeable claim to fame: in a small and unobtrusive house on its outskirts, now marked by a plaque, the man who was to become Lawrence of Arabia was born, in August 1888.

Below Tan-yr-Allt, near the road, Madocks brought about the first introduction of the Industrial Revolution into North Wales, in 1805, in the form of a water mill, which may still be seen, though now in disrepair. It was somewhere near this point that the old route set off across the sands.

The new land around Tremadog proved fertile, and the success of this first venture encouraged him to go further. He set about buying up the coastal lands of the estuary in order to be able to bring to reality Sir John Wynn's ambitious idea. An enclosure Bill of 1806 at first failed to gain support, and only on the third attempt did he succeed in gaining the necessary legislation for the great embankment to become a reality.

It was finished in July 1811, at a final cost of over £60,000, and left Madocks heavily in debt and greatly in need of revenue from the resulting land. This aim received a sharp set-back in February, 1812, when an exceptional storm breached it. Help and support were raised from the whole neighbourhood, but there was still a desperate need for funds, and Madocks was now greatly financially embarrassed and hounded by creditors. His personal possessions were sold to pay off part of one enormous debt, and he was forced to transfer his lands into other ownerships and let them to his main creditor.

A surprising addition to the whole remarkable story is the arrival in the area of the poet Shelley with his young wife. Then aged only nineteen and not yet famous, he had expectations of inheritance and was romantically inclined to causes such as Madocks' reclamation scheme. He joined in the fund-raising, and subsequently became the tenant of Tan-yr-Allt. The

Shelleys eventually left the area suddenly after an apparent attack on them, and the debts they left behind added to the distrust already established by those of Madocks.

In the meantime the repair of the embankment took place against all these odds. Madocks' finances revived through a fortunate marriage, and he was able to re-acquire his property and to be involved in the final phases of his grand scheme, the railway along the embankment and its destination, the quays of Port Madoc. He died before all this reached fulfilment, however, returning from a holiday in Italy, in Paris, in September 1828. His life had the heroic quality of which myth is made, and this feature extends to the story current at the time that he had not really died but returned, in disguise, like Glyndŵr, to live out the remainder of his life in obscurity.

One result of the embankment was the diversion of the River Glaslyn, and quite accidentally an effect of this was the carving out of a deep channel which made a potential new harbour. Parliamentary consent was acquired to develop this, and the construction of 'Port Madoc' was started in 1821, completed in 1824 (25). The name, now adapted to a more authentic Welsh form, was laid down in a Parliamentary Act of 1821, which gave its founder, Madocks, the right to dues, and to the appointment of a harbour-master, in recognition of his funding of the harbour works. Samuel Holland, the quarry owner, acquired a quay in the new harbour, and the development of the railway line from Ffestiniog to there was largely his scheme.

There was considerable local opposition to this, since the business of freighting slates by cart and boat on the Dwyryd provided employment. Holland however got his railway bill through Parliament and the construction started in 1833. Its thirteen miles were finished in 1836, having cost some £6,000.

It was at first a gravitational tramway, the cars pulled back up by horses which then rode down in one of them. Nearly thirty years later steam locomotives became practical, and it has been driven by steam since 1836.

Port Madoc thrived in a way neither Madocks nor Holland could have predicted. The price of slate continued to rise with the building boom, and the repeal of the slate tax in 1831 boosted it further. The population of the new port rose equivalently from the 1830's to the 1850's, and it doubled again between 1851 and 1881. This led to slum conditions in some parts of the town, and in the 1850's there were problems of epidemics and overcrowding.

The sound home market for slate in the meantime enabled the opening up of exports, and Port Madoc started to ship slate to Liverpool for onward transport to Australia, and directly to the ports of Germany, where much building was also taking place at that time. Hamburg, for instance, is almost entirely roofed by Ffestiniog slate shipped from Port Madoc. Further lowering and abolition of tariffs led to a market in France and Scandinavia, and the slates went from Hamburg (which remained Port Madoc's major destination) on into central Europe. A less frequent trade meanwhile developed with America.

Ship-building had been traditional in the area since the 18th century, particularly at Pwllheli, where 260 vessels were built between 1759 and 1824. The vast increase in export trade now gave rise to a major ship-building industry at Port Madoc. The techniques used were traditional, and in fact by then old-fashioned – everything was made on the spot by local craftsmen – but the result was remarkably effective. It is generally acknowledged that Port Madoc schooners were of very superior quality (26).

Three-masted vessels, characterised by a slanted bow, with fore-and-aft, rather than square-rigged, sails (which allowed them to beat to windward and thus to be able to make short tacks away from a lee shore beset with obstructions) they were strongly built and more than adequate for the slate trade in which they were mainly employed. It was a form specifically developed to cope with the sudden build-up of short, high waves off the south-Caernarfonshire coast and the strong landward drift of tidal current which made progress hard and hazardous for squatter vessels.

In their last, fully-developed form, a type called Western Ocean Yachts, the schooners reached a peak of refinement, evoking adoring praise from all experts, no less for their beauty and elegance than for their perfection of efficiency.

At a peak in 1873 Port Madoc exported 116,567 tons of slate. A slight lull was followed by a revival in the 1880's, and the early 1890's saw Port Madoc's last and greatest period of ship-building in full flow. The industry then involved the whole town, and the launch of a new schooner was an event which everybody turned out to celebrate. The slate industry declined from 1903, and the schooners largely traded fish and imported commodities from Liverpool and Ireland. Many of the later ships were sold to new owners in Newfoundland, where they ended their days. The German connection continued well into this century, but was brought to an abrupt close, and with it the boom days of Port Madoc, with the start of the Great War in August 1914.

INTO OUR TIMES

THIS area has been rich not only in history but also in personalities who have affected history. Porthmadog would never have had its time of flowering, the impact of which had been felt in places as diverse as Hamburg and Newfoundland, if it had not been for the occurrence there of individuals as remarkable as Madocks and Holland. It is almost incredible that at the same time, the late 19th century, a personality and career was develping only six or so miles away which was to have an influence in an even greater field.

David Lloyd George was not actually born at Llanystumdwy, the village just west of Cricieth, but there and Cricieth were home for him from his infancy until his death, a span of 82 years. He was born in 1836 at New York Place, Chorlton-upon-Medlock, Manchester, where a plaque on a nearby house commemorates this event. His parents were of course Welsh, his father William George a schoolmaster originally from Pembrokeshire, who died when David was only eighteen months old. His mother (nèe Elizabeth Lloyd, the source of his double surname) moved with the child and his elder sister Mary Ellen back to Llanystumdwy where her brother lived, and Lloyd George was brought up in his house.

Richard, 'Uncle Lloyd', was a shoemaker and a part-time Baptist minister, and he evidently had the traditional Welsh respect for education since he coached the young Lloyd George and instilled in him the radical principles which are an essential part of Welsh values. David's formal education was limited to Llanystumdwy village school, which he left at thirteen. Shortly after the family's move a younger brother, William, was born. A plaque now identifies the cottage, across the road from the Feathers Inn, where they lived.

When he was sixteen Lloyd George joined a firm of solicitors in Porthmadog as an articled clerk, and five years later, in 1884 (having passed his law exams), he formed his own practice in Cricieth, later in Porthmadog, and continued as a solicitor in partnership with his brother for the next five years. From the start a dedicated politician, he was elected to the newly-formed Caernarfonshire County Council in 1888, and in that same year gained the nomination to the local Parliamentary seat. In 1890 the death of the conservative member presented him with the opportunity of a by-election. He was twenty-seven when he contested, and won, the seat of Caernarfon Boroughs, by a margin of only eighteen votes.

Lloyd George's interest in politics was primarily nationalistic, and he became a Liberal because the Welsh Nationalists had sided with the Liberal

(27) Curnow Vosper's painting 'Salem'

(28) The Lloyd George memorial at Llanystumdwy

(29) Abersoch

Party in support of their policy of Welsh disestablishment. Lloyd George's nationalistic ambitions at that time went further than this non-conformist aim, since he wanted complete home rule. He was already a founder member of Cymru Fydd, the early form of the present Plaid Cymru, the nationalist party. Radicalism, nationalism and non-conformity are interlinked, and we have to remember that this is very much a chapel-based area. It is perhaps appropriate that the stereotyped depiction of Welsh tradition, Curnow Vosper's painting 'Salem', is actually based on Salem Chapel in the Nantcol valley behind Llanbedr in southern Gwynedd (27).

Undoubtedly Lloyd George's radical principles had a lasting effect on British politics. He rose from these unpropitious beginnings at Llanystumdwy to become Chancellor of the Exchequer and then Prime Minister, from 1916 to 1922, the time of the First World War and its aftermath. Throughout his renowned career as national leader he remained true to his roots, and he held the same Caernarfon seat for fifty-five years. When illness forced him to retire in 1931 he returned to live in Cricieth, in a house called Bryn Awelon, on the north side of the town, and is buried back at Llanystumdwy, beside the attractive river Dwyfor, near where a memorial museum houses mementoes of his life (28). Two months before he died he resigned his seat to accept a peerage, characteristically taking his title from his home region, Earl Lloyd-George of Dwyfor.

During the period of Lloyd George's rise, Porthmadog's decline, and Britain's adjustment to the 20th century and our modern times, Llŷn, like everywhere else, had been slowly changing. Seaside resorts were an invention of the 19th century, a new middle class forming the habit of taking holidays in other parts of their own country, seeking scenery and health-giving seaside air. As Pwllheli declined as a port it rose as a beach resort, served from 1867 by the Cambrian Coast Railway from Barmouth. The beach itself had been improved by the effects of drainage, and its new role had developed fast from the second decade of the 19th century. The 'Yr Hafan' marina complex continues this area's long connection with ships and the sea into modern times.

Cricieth likewise benefited greatly by the coming of the railway, but their contemporary ancient borough, Nefyn, was deprived of this advantage and left somewhat out on a limb by the eventual rejection of Porth Dinllaen as the port of Ireland. A two-mile stretch of sand at Morfa Nefyn compensates for this isolation, and indeed all down the coast there are justly famous beaches, such as Porth Oer, the 'Whistling Sands' near Aberdaron, Porth

Neigwl, known as 'Hell's Mouth', to its east, and on the other side of the peninsula Morfa Bychan near Porthmadog and Black Rock sands.

One of the most successful of these small resorts is undoubtedly Abersoch (29), near the peninsula's eastern tip, sheltered from prevailing winds and intimately enclosed by headlands. Its rise from fishing-village to major yacht harbour is a phenomenon of the last few decades, and it thrives now as a small-boat haven, its main focus being its yacht club. Down at the peninsula's end the island of Bardsey has once again become something of a destination for modern pilgrims, with trips to its world of seabirds and peace, controlled by the Bardsey Trust, becoming increasingly popular.